METAL

Gareth Stevens Publishing
A WORLD ALMANAC EDUCATION GROUP COMPANY

Please visit our web site at: www.garethstevens.com
For a free color catalog describing Gareth Stevens Publishing's
list of high-quality books and multimedia programs,
call 1-800-542-2595 (USA) or 1-800-387-3178 (Canada).
Gareth Stevens Publishing's fax: (414) 332-3567.

Library of Congress Cataloging-in-Publication Data

Metal.
    p. cm. — (Let's create!)
    Includes bibliographical references.
    Summary: Step-by-step instructions for twelve craft projects, including glasses, a magnetic
butterfly, and a thumbtack mosaic, using various common metal objects such as bottle caps,
aluminum foil and trays, cans, and paper clips.
    ISBN 0-8368-4016-X (lib. bdg.)
    1. Scrap metals—Recycling—Juvenile literature.   2. Metal-work—Juvenile literature.
3. Wire craft—Juvenile literature.   4. Tin cans—Juvenile literature.   [1. Metalwork.
2. Handicraft.]   I. Title.   II. Series.
TT214.M4813   2004
745.56—dc22   2003057388

This North American edition first published in 2004 by
Gareth Stevens Publishing
A World Almanac Education Group Company
330 West Olive Street, Suite 100
Milwaukee, WI 53212 USA

First published as *¡Vamos a crear! Metales* with an original copyright © 2002 by
Parramón Ediciones, S.A., – World Rights, text and illustrations by Parramón's
Editorial Team. This U.S. edition copyright © 2004 by Gareth Stevens, Inc.
Additional end matter copyright © 2004 by Gareth Stevens, Inc.

English Translation: Colleen Coffey
Gareth Stevens Series Editor: Dorothy L. Gibbs
Gareth Stevens Designer: Katherine A. Goedheer

Printed in Spain

1 2 3 4 5 6 7 8 9 08 07 06 05 04

Table of Contents

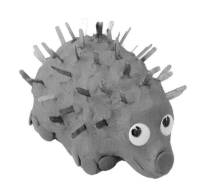

Introduction

Metals are both old and modern materials. Ever since their discovery, back in prehistoric times, they have been useful to human beings, and, little by little, they have become very necessary in our lives.

Aluminum, brass, copper, nickel, steel, and tin are some of the metals found in objects we use every day. Look around you. In your kitchen alone, you will find bottle caps, pots and pans, food and soft drink cans, aluminum foil, and scouring pads.

Crafts made with metals can be useful, decorative, and fun. This book presents twelve craft projects made with paper clips, thumbtacks, aluminum and tin cans, foil pans, brass fasteners, and many other easy-to-find metal objects. You just have to gather the objects — and create!

Use a soft drink can to make a Musical Maraca. Create magnetic Fishing Fun with pizza pans, paper clips, food cans, and wire. Design a Thumbtack Mosaic or turn an aluminum bread pan and a few jar lids into a Big Shiny Bus.

Besides being easy to find, the metal objects you will need for the projects in this book are also easy to use. These crafts do not require metals that need special adhesives to put together or metals that will cut you. Be sure, however, to ask an adult for help with food cans that might have sharp edges. The only wire you will need is the thin, flexible kind that is easy to shape and can be cut with a pair of scissors.

Most of the other tools you will need to make the metal crafts in this book are things you use every day at home or at school, including glue, tape, scissors, and paints.

Watch for special instructions at the end of each project to try other great ideas. Sometimes, making just one small change creates a very different result.

Metal crafts are lots of fun, and you'll beam with pride when your project's done.

Smiley Sunshine

The lid of a jar is the perfect metal object for making any of the heavenly orbs in our solar system. Why not start with the Sun?

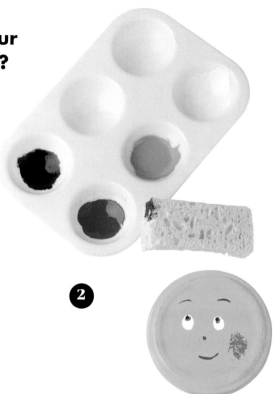

1 Paint a medium-size, round, metal jar lid yellow-orange.

2 When the yellow-orange paint is dry, use black, white, green, and red paints to make a face that has eyebrows, eyes, a nose, and a mouth. Finish the face by using a sponge to dab on red paint for cheeks.

You will need:
- yellow-orange, black, white, green, and red paints
- paintbrush
- medium-size, round, metal jar lid
- sponge
- scissors
- flexible gold wire
- black tape

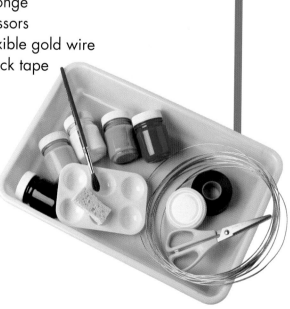

3 Cut four pieces of gold wire, making each piece about 6 inches (15 centimeters) long.

6

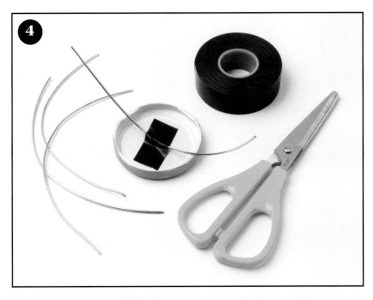

4 Use strong black tape to attach each piece of wire to the back side of the painted lid. Arrange the pieces of wire to look like a star.

5 Shape the ends of each wire around the rim of the painted lid to look like sun rays.

Brighten your bedroom by hanging this smiley-face sunshine on the wall!

Another Great Idea!
Paint the metal jar lid to look like the body of a big brown spider. Shape the ends of the wires differently to make the spider's eight legs.

Three-in-a-Row Game

This entertaining game is tick-tack-toe with a twist. The playing pieces won't fall off the board! Metal and magnets are the key.

1 With a black marker, trace around the bottom of a small aluminum pan on a piece of orange poster board, then cut out the figure.

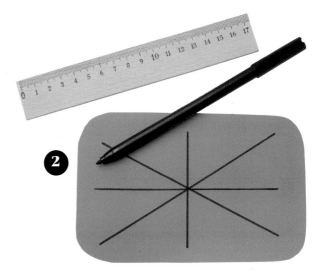

2 Using a ruler and a black marker, draw four lines to make an eight-pointed star.

You will need:
- black marker
- small, rectangular aluminum pan
- orange poster board
- scissors
- ruler
- self-adhesive magnets
- yellow and green paints
- paintbrush
- 6 bottle caps
- glue stick

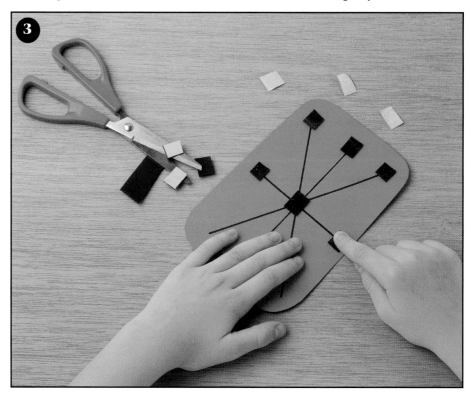

3 Cut nine small pieces of self-adhesive magnets. Stick one piece of magnet at the end of each point of the star and one more in the center, where all the lines cross.

4 Paint six bottle caps, making three of them yellow and the other three green.

5 Place the aluminum pan upside down and glue the orange game board to the bottom of it. The side with the magnets should be facing upward.

You can play Three-in-a-Row almost anywhere. The magnets hold the metal playing pieces securely in place.

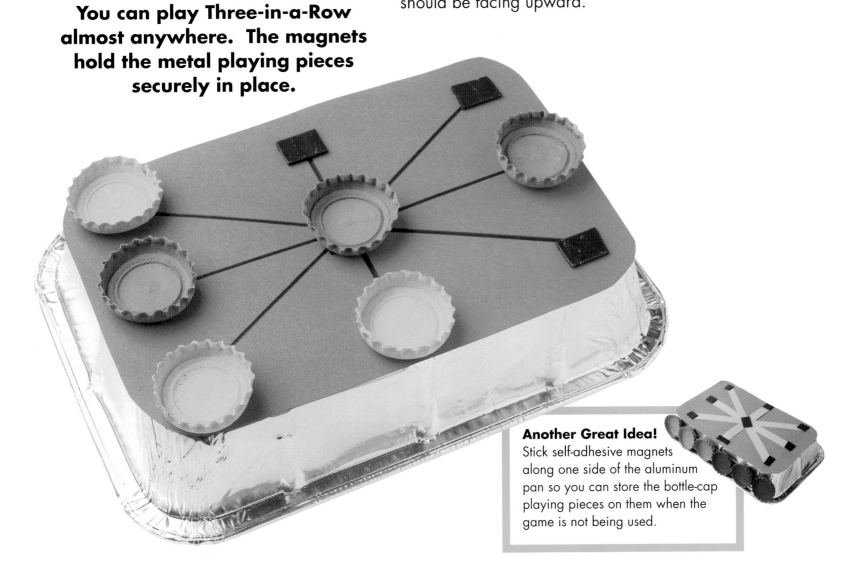

Another Great Idea!
Stick self-adhesive magnets along one side of the aluminum pan so you can store the bottle-cap playing pieces on them when the game is not being used.

Musical Maraca

This musical instrument is as easy to make as it is to play. So make it — then shake it!

1 Pour uncooked rice into a clean, empty soft drink can that has been painted red. Cover the opening of the can with colored tape.

2 Mix instant papier-mâché powder with a little water until it forms a paste.

3 Use the paste to attach a narrow cardboard tube to the painted can.

4 When the papier-mâché paste is dry, paint it red to match the color of the soft drink can. Then, paint the cardboard tube orange and paint a red stripe around the end of it.

10

6 Decorate your maraca by sticking colored thumb-tacks into the large polka dots on the papier-mâché.

5 Paint orange and white stripes over the red paint on the soft drink can and paint large and small orange and white polka dots over the red paint on the papier-mâché paste.

Make another maraca so you can shake and rattle a rhythm with both hands!

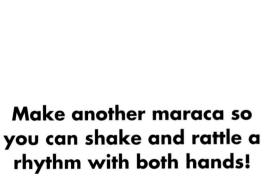

Another Great Idea!
For a different sound, make your maracas out of covered plastic containers and put beans inside.

Thumbtack Mosaic

With metal thumbtacks, making a mosaic couldn't be easier. For a dazzling design, use lots of bright colors.

1 With black marker, on a square piece of cork, draw a plant that has four flowers.

2 Stick silver thumbtacks along all four edges of the cork to make a frame.

You will need:
- black marker
- square piece of cork
- silver, green, red, white, orange, blue, and yellow thumbtacks

3 Stick green thumbtacks across the base line under the plant and on all of the flower stems.

4 To make each of the four flowers, use a thumbtack of one color surrounded by six thumbtacks of another color.

**Done already?
It was easy,
wasn't it?**

Another Great Idea!
Fill in the background of your mosaic with more colored thumbtacks or create new mosaics of drawings, letters, or numbers in any design you desire.

Fishing Fun

Combining different types of metal objects makes this magnetic fishing game fun to put together and even more fun to play with.

1 With a pair of scissors, make eight cuts across a round aluminum pizza pan to create four aluminum strips. The cuts should be equally spaced around the pan and should not reach the center of the pan. Cover the four aluminum strips with purple crepe paper, using a glue stick to attach it.

2 Glue the cut pizza pan inside another pizza pan of exactly the same shape and size. Bend the purple strips so that they look like waves in the ocean.

3 Bend pieces of flexible blue wire into spirals that will be used to represent the water in the ocean.

4 With a black marker, draw six fish on a piece of white paper. Color the fish with colored pencils, then cut the fish out.

5 Attach each fish to a metal bottle cap with glue stick.

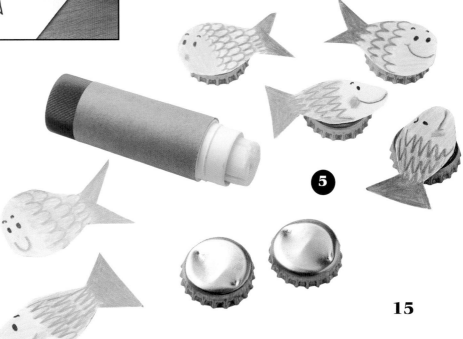

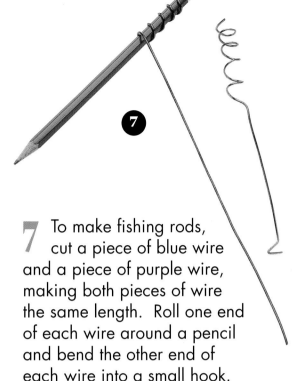

6 Place the fish and the water spirals in the pizza pan "ocean."

7 To make fishing rods, cut a piece of blue wire and a piece of purple wire, making both pieces of wire the same length. Roll one end of each wire around a pencil and bend the other end of each wire into a small hook.

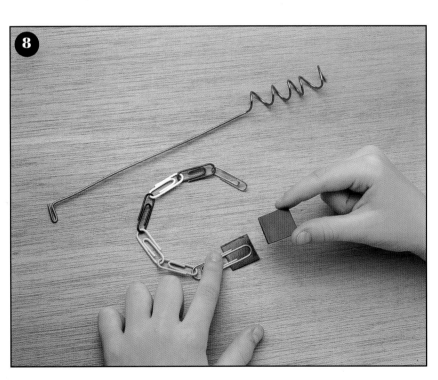

8 Make two chains out of colored metal paper clips and stick together two pieces of self-adhesive magnet over a paper clip at one end of each chain. The paper-clip chains are fishing lines, the magnets are hooks. Hang a line from each fishing rod by attaching the open end of a paper-clip chain to the small hook on each wire rod.

9 Draw the number 1 on a piece of blue poster board and the number 2 on orange poster board, then cut out both numbers.

10 Attach each number to a separate metal food can with glue stick. These cans are where each player will keep the fish he or she catches.

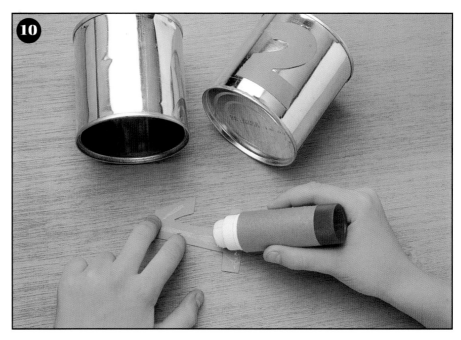

Invite a friend to join you for some fishing fun. The player who catches more fish is the winner.

Another Great Idea!
Make all different kinds of fish and other sea creatures and give each creature a certain number of points. In this game, the player who has more points is the winner.

Wire Windmill

You can turn this simple, aluminum-and-wire windmill into an original work of art. All it takes is some paint and a little imagination.

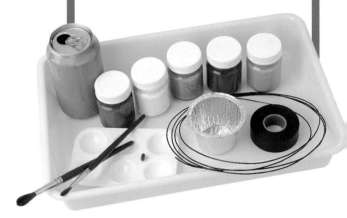

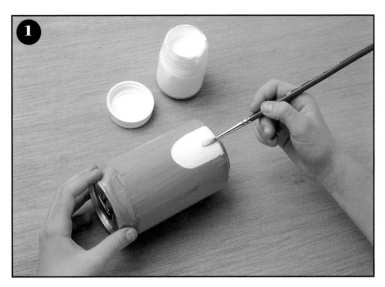

1 Paint a white door and two white windows on a clean, empty soft drink can that has been painted pink.

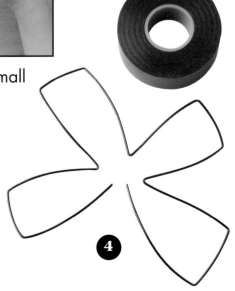

2 Using green, orange, white, and red paints, decorate the can with grass and flowers. Then, paint blue stripes on the door and a blue border around the windows.

3 To make a roof, paint a small aluminum muffin cup red.

4 Use a piece of flexible black wire to shape the blades of the windmill. Fasten the ends of the wire together, in the center of the blades, with black tape.

18

5 Attach the blades to the painted can with a red thumbtack and push the roof onto the top of the can.

If you're careful, you will be able to rotate the blades of the windmill.

Another Great Idea!
Paint another soft drink can a different color and do not attach any blades. Then you will have a beautiful house to decorate any way you like.

Big Shiny Bus

A bread-pan bus is so easy to make it will be ready for passengers in no time. Ready . . . set . . . glue!

1 Cut four circles out of purple paper. The circles should be smaller than the metal jar lids you will be using. Use glue stick to attach a circle to the center of each lid, on the outside of the lid.

2 With liquid school glue, attach a brass paper fastener to the center of each metal jar lid, on the inside of the lid. The lids are the wheels of the bus.

3 Use another brass paper fastener to poke holes into each long side of an aluminum bread pan, making one hole in the front and one in the back. Stick a wheel into each hole and bend back the ends of the paper fastener.

4 On a sheet of white paper, draw two long strips of windows for the sides of the bread pan and two small windows, one for the front and one for the back. Use colored pencils to draw a passenger in each of the windows.

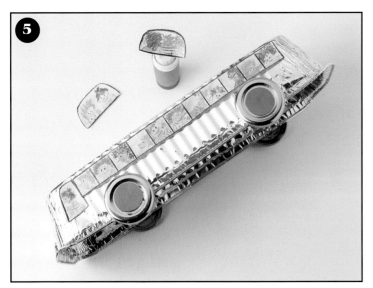

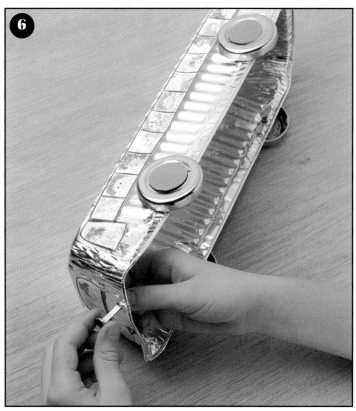

5 Cut out the two strips of windows and the front and back windows. Glue all of the windows onto the aluminum bread pan.

6 Poke two brass paper fasteners into the front of the bus, under the front window, to make headlights.

Is everybody on board? The big shiny bus is ready to roll!

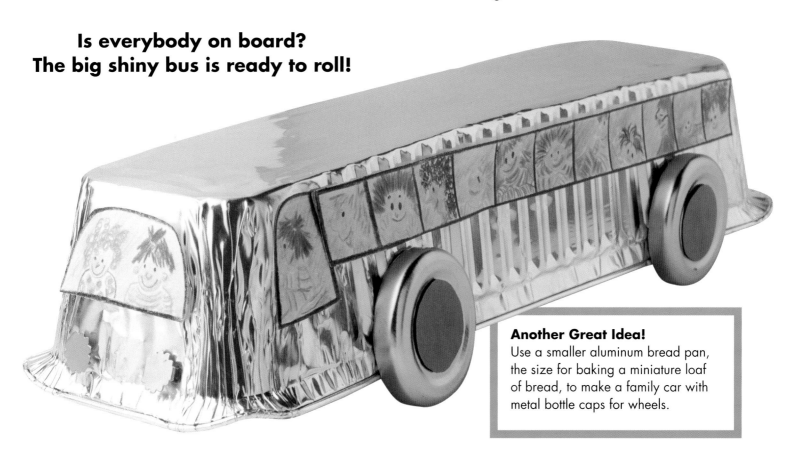

Another Great Idea!
Use a smaller aluminum bread pan, the size for baking a miniature loaf of bread, to make a family car with metal bottle caps for wheels.

Nutty Necklace

Did you ever think of using hardware to create elegant jewelry? Follow these instructions to see how easily you can make a pretty necklace out of metal nuts, wooden beads, and a piece of wire.

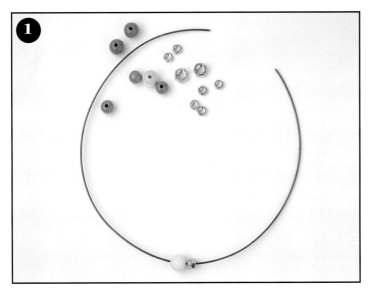

1 Thread one light brown wooden bead and two small metal nuts onto a long piece of flexible red wire.

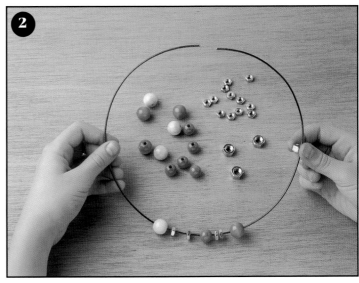

2 Then, thread on one pink bead and two more small nuts, followed by one orange bead and one large metal nut.

You will need:
- light brown, pink, and orange wooden beads
- small and large metal nuts
- flexible red wire
- yellow tape

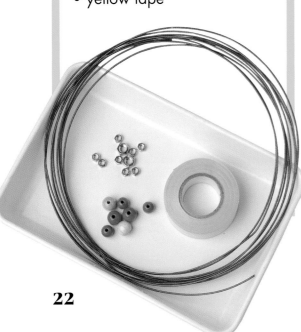

3 Repeat step 2, then finish with one pink bead, two small nuts, and one light brown bead.

3

4 Cover both ends of the red wire with yellow tape so they do not rub against your neck. Bend the ends of the wire into small hooks to form a clasp.

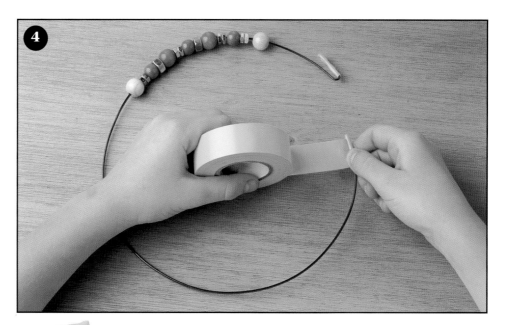

Your beautiful nut-and-bead necklace is ready to wear. Do you see how the metal nuts sparkle?

Another Great Idea!
Use different combinations of bead colors with both steel and brass nuts to design necklaces that will match different outfits.

Bouncy Buddy

In crafty hands, a piece of wire can spring to life. Add a friendly face, and you've got yourself a new pal. This one's a real doll.

You will need:
- flexible purple wire
- narrow cardboard tube
- black marker
- small cork ball
- 2 aluminum muffin cups
- modeling clay
- scissors
- silver thumbtack

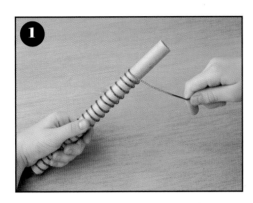

1 Wrap a piece of flexible purple wire around a narrow cardboard tube to form a spiral, then slide the spiral off of the tube.

2 Using a black marker, draw a face on a small cork ball.

3 Fill an aluminum muffin cup with modeling clay. The clay can be any color. Turn the clay-filled muffin cup upside down to use as a base.

4 Stick one end of the wire spiral into the clay-filled base and stick the other end into the cork-ball head.

5 Cut another aluminum muffin cup in half and cut two strips off of one half to make arms for the spiral doll. Cut slits into the rest of the half muffin cup to make hair.

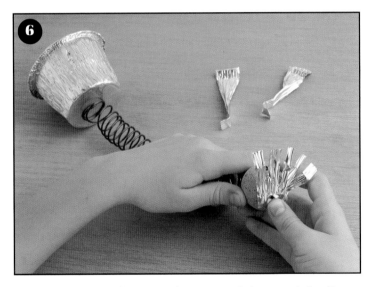

6 Attach the hair to the top of the cork-ball head with a silver thumbtack. Fold each aluminum arm strip over slightly, at the narrow end, and wrap it around the first coil in the wire spiral, just below the doll's head.

Give him a nudge and Buddy will bounce up and down and totter back and forth.

Another Great Idea!
Use a Styrofoam ball instead of a cork ball to make the doll's head and use colored markers to make the face.

Magnetic Butterfly

This shiny butterfly will stick around all year long — on your refrigerator or any other metal surface. It's magnetic!

You will need:
- black marker
- rectangular aluminum cake pan
- scissors
- violet and green paper
- glue stick
- fine-tipped black marker
- self-adhesive magnet

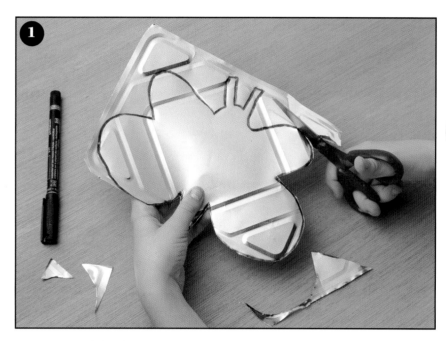

1 Use a black marker to draw the shape of a butterfly on the bottom of a rectangular aluminum cake pan. Cut out the aluminum butterfly with a pair of scissors.

2 Draw two large and two small circles on violet paper, then draw two large and two small circles on green paper. Make the green circles smaller than the violet circles. Cut out all of the circles. Glue the violet circles onto the butterfly's wings. Glue the green circles on top of the violet circles.

3 Use a fine-tipped black marker to draw the body of the butterfly on green paper and to draw a face on the butterfly's head, then cut out the butterfly's body.

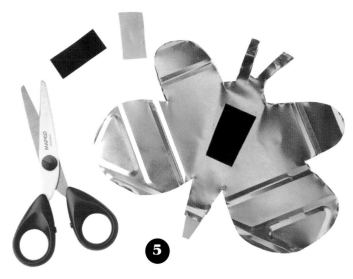

4 Cut narrow strips of violet paper. Glue the violet strips across the butterfly's body and glue the body between the wings on the aluminum butterfly.

5 Cut a wide strip of self-adhesive magnet and stick it onto the back of the aluminum butterfly, between the wings.

Unlike most other insects, this one will be welcome in any room of the house.

Another Great Idea!
Make more magnets in other shapes. Try making a ship or an ice cream cone.

Purple Porcupine

The pointed ends of brass paper fasteners look a lot like the quills that make a porcupine prickly. Just for fun, make your prickly porcupine purple.

You will need:
- purple modeling clay
- small brass paper fasteners
- white, orange, and green thumbtacks
- black marker

1 Shape a large lump of purple modeling clay into the body of a porcupine.

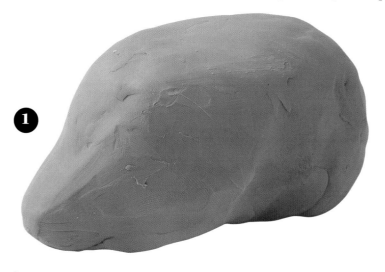

2 To make the porcupine's quills, press lots of brass paper fasteners into the clay so that only the points are showing. Cover the back and sides of the porcupine with brass "quills."

3 Use two white thumbtacks for eyes and draw pupils on them with a black marker.

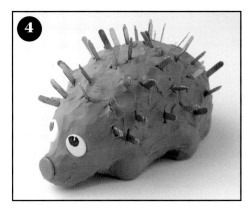

4 Stick the eyes onto the porcupine's face and stick an orange thumbtack at the end of its nose.

5 Finish the porcupine by sticking three green thumbtacks in each of its four feet to make claws.

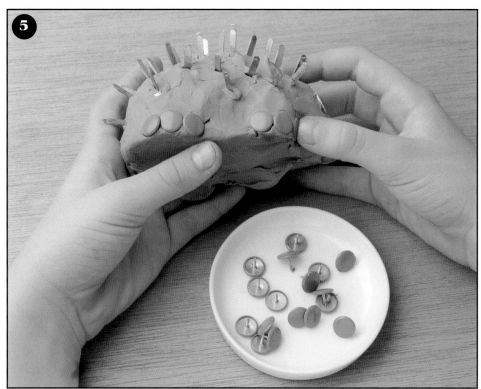

Be careful! Don't let this purple porcupine's sharp quills prick you!

Another Great Idea!
Shape modeling clay into the head of a man and use paper fasteners for his hair.

29

Spectacular Specs

With these good-looking eyeglasses, you can see your way around in style — and you don't need many materials to make them!

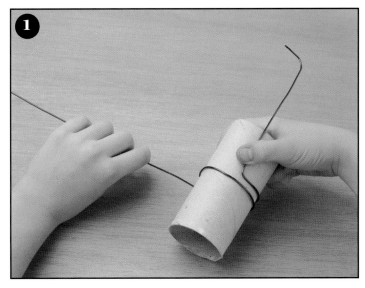

1 Cut a long piece of flexible purple wire. Bend one end of the wire to shape a bow that will fit over your ear, then wrap the wire around a cardboard toilet paper tube to make one of the lens frames.

2 Use the cardboard tube again to shape the other lens frame.

You will need:
- scissors
- flexible purple wire
- cardboard toilet paper tube
- bright green tape

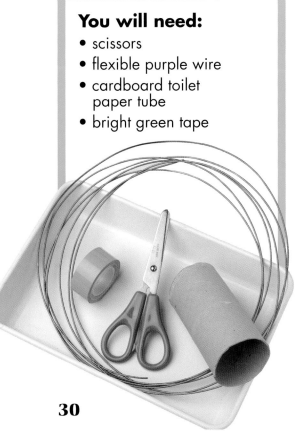

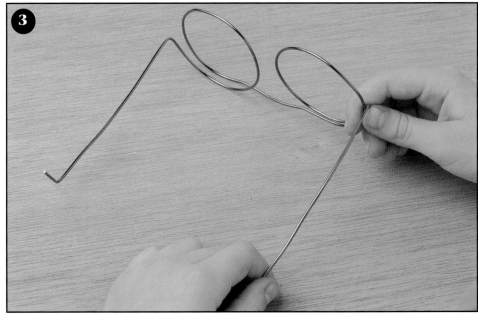

3 Remove the cardboard tube and shape another bow to fit over your other ear. Cut the end of the wire, if necessary, to make the two bows even.

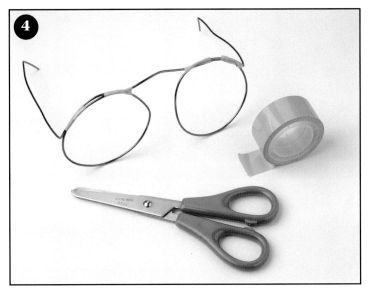

4 Cut small pieces of bright green tape and wrap them around the tops of the two lens frames to hold the wire loops together.

5 Add more pieces of bright green tape, spaced evenly apart, on the bows and on the lower part of the lens frames. Wrap the end of each bow with tape, too, so the wire will not poke you behind your ears.

These spectacles might not help you see better, but you will look good wearing them.

Another Great Idea!
Shape the lens frames around square or rectangular cardboard boxes instead of a cardboard tube and use different colors of wire and tape to create a variety of fashionable eyewear.

Glossary

beam: (v) to smile joyfully

bow: (n) the side piece of an eyeglasses frame that reaches from the lens back to the ear

flexible: able to be bent

hardware: tools and related items, such as screws, nuts, bolts, and washers, that are made of metal

mosaic: a type of art work in which small pieces of a hard, colorful material are fitted together to form a design

nudge: (n) a light push

orbs: round or circular objects; spheres

pupils: the round, dark spots in the center of the colored parts of people's eyes

quills: sharp, needlelike spines on the bodies of porcupines and hedgehogs

rotate: to turn or move in a circle

self-adhesive: able to stick to another surface without using glue or tape

spirals: continuous series of circular turns that are usually the same size; coils

totter: rock unsteadily from side to side

More Books to Read

Foil Fun. Let's Start! (series). Wayne South and Todd South (Silver Dolphin Books)

Funky Junk. Kids Can Do It (series). Renée Schwarz (Kids Can Press)

Paper Clip Jewelry! Kelli Peduzzi (Pleasant Company)

Pie Pan Mania. Craft Mania (series). Christine M. Irvin (Children's Book Press)

Snappy Jazzy Jewelry. Katie Gayle (Sterling)

Wire Art for Kids Ages 5–95! Can Do Crafts (series). Suzanne McNeill (Design Originals)

Web Sites

Bee Bird House. www.geocities.com/ twilagail/beebirdhouse.html

Reuse Bottles, Jars, and Cans. www.kidsdomain.com/craft/_recjarcan.html